Mapping Earthforms

Mountains

Catherine Chambers

Heinemann
LIBRARY

First published in Great Britain by Heinemann Library,
Halley Court, Jordan Hill, Oxford OX2 8EJ,
a division of Reed Educational and Professional Publishing Ltd.
Heinemann is a registered trademark of Reed Educational & Professional Publishing Limited.

OXFORD MELBOURNE AUCKLAND
JOHANNESBURG BLANTYRE GABORONE
IBADAN PORTSMOUTH NH (USA) CHICAGO

Designed by David Oakley
Illustrations by Tokay Interactive Ltd
Originated by Dot Gradations
Printed in Hong Kong/China

04 03 02 01 00
10 9 8 7 6 5 4 3 2 1

ISBN 0 431 09845 X

British Library Cataloguing in Publication Data

Chambers, Catherine
    Mountains. – (Mapping earthforms)
    1. Mountain ecology – Juvenile literature 2. Mountains – Maps –
    Juvenile literature
    I. Title
    577.5'3

Acknowledgements
The Publishers would like to thank the following for permission to reproduce photographs: Ardea: B Gibbons p17; Bruce Coleman Collection: J Grande pp18, 19; Ecoscene: A Brown p15; Robert Harding Picture Library: pp4, 20, S Harris p12; Anthony King: p13; Oxford Scientific Films: K Su p23, D and M Plage p27, G Merlen p29; Popperfoto: p26; G R Roberts: pp6, 21, 25; South American Pictures: p10; Still Pictures: S Noorani p24; Survival Anglia: Konrad Wothe p5.

Cover photograph reproduced with permission of Robert Harding Picture Library.

Every effort has been made to contact copyright holders of any material reproduced in this book. Any omissions will be rectified in subsequent printings if notice is given to the Publisher.

For more information about Heinemann Library books, or to order, please phone ++44 (0)1865 888066, or send a fax to ++44 (0)1865 314091. You can visit our website at www.heinemann.co.uk.

Any words appearing in the text in bold, **like this,** are explained in the Glossary.

Contents

What is a mountain?

A mountain is a huge, steep-sided rock formation that rises above the Earth's surface. Some people think that a real mountain on dry land has to rise at least 1000 metres above sea level. Others believe that the exact height does not matter.

Many mountains occur in a long chain, or **range**. Each **peak** in the range is often described as a separate mountain. Mountains can lie under the oceans – rising from the sea bed. Some stick out above the oceans. Others cannot be seen at all.

How are mountains formed?

Mountains are made in three main ways. The first is when the **plates** of the Earth's crust are pushed together or upwards, making the surface rock crumple and fold. The second

Uluru is a sandstone rock in central Australia. It is massive – 6 km (3.75 mi) long and 2 km (1.25 mi) wide. But it is only 348 m high, so many people call it a rock, not a mountain. What do you think it is? When the sun sets, the light makes Uluru change to a rich red colour. Uluru is a sacred place for the Aboriginal peoples of Australia. It attracts many tourists too.

is when areas of soft rock are worn away, leaving peaks or **plateaux** of harder rock sticking out. The third main way is when hot, soft rock from under the Earth's crust shoots through gaps in the Earth's crust. It rises in a cone and cools into a volcanic mountain. We shall learn more about how different kinds of mountain are formed.

Mountains often make borders between countries. But the Ural Mountains in this picture separate two very different cultures in just one country. To the west lies European Russia; to the east lies Asian Russia.

What do mountains look like?

Mountains give the world some of its most amazing scenery. The rocks give many different shapes, patterns and colours. A very high mountain can look lush and green at its foot. It can be rocky and covered with snow at its peak. We shall discover more about the great variety of mountain landscapes.

Life on the mountains

Life on the mountains can be tough, especially high up. But many plants have adapted to the cold winds and poor soils. Creatures have learned to survive in the thin air and thick snow – so have people. But there are many other types of soil and **climate** on the mountains, as we shall find out. We shall also see what the future holds for life in the mountains.

The world's mountains

Where in the world?

Mountains occur all over the world and in many different **environments**. Occasionally, single **peaks** and **ridges** rise suddenly above flat ground. Some are islands that seem to pop up out of the sea. A lot of these are underwater volcanoes and lie largely in parts of the Pacific Ocean.

But most mountains rise in **ranges**. These are often found on the edges of great land masses, called **continents**. Each range has a cluster of peaks, ridges and **valleys** that were all formed at the same time and in a similar way. Ranges are often separated by a high, flat stretch of rock called a **plateau**.

Groups of ranges are called a mountain system or chain. But there are even bigger groups than this! They are known as a **belt**, or **cordillera**. The biggest belts on land are the Himalayas in central Asia, the Rockies

The Great Dividing Range stretches down the east of Australia. It causes rain, brought by constant winds, to fall on the east side. To the west lies the Great Australian Desert.

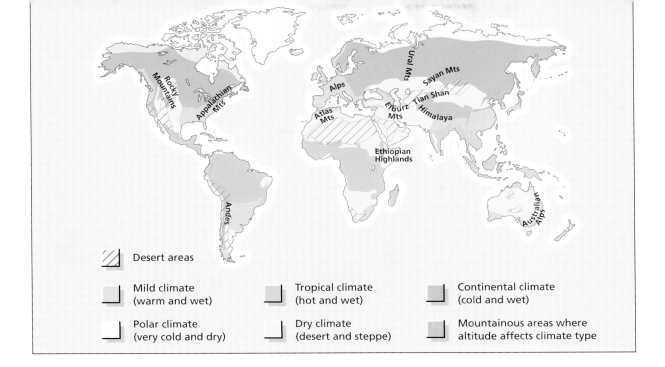

Desert areas

Mild climate (warm and wet)

Tropical climate (hot and wet)

Continental climate (cold and wet)

Polar climate (very cold and dry)

Dry climate (desert and steppe)

Mountainous areas where altitude affects climate type

in North America and the Andes in South America. Even longer cordilleras can be found in the world's oceans.

Mountains and climates

Mountains occur in all kinds of **climate**, from the frozen lands of Alaska to the hot deserts of the Sahara. But mountains themselves can have a big effect on weather.

Winds blow rain clouds on to continents. When the clouds meet mountain ranges, they rise up them and shed their rain. But the rain rarely reaches the other side. This is why so many deserts lie on one side of a mountain range. The deserts are in what is known as rain-shadow areas. Mountains shape the weather around them too. Ranges make their own small climate zones. These affect the plants, creatures and people that live on the slopes.

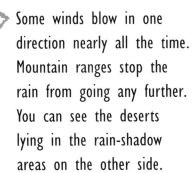 Some winds blow in one direction nearly all the time. Mountain ranges stop the rain from going any further. You can see the deserts lying in the rain-shadow areas on the other side.

How are mountains formed?

The moving Earth

Mountains are formed mostly because the Earth moves! The **continents** rest on seven huge pieces of the Earth's crust, called **plates**. The plates move about on a swaying layer of boiling hot, sticky rock. This layer is known as the **mantle**. Many of the world's mountains were formed millions of years ago when the plates bumped together and slid apart. Mountains are still slowly rising and changing shape as the plates continue to shift. This movement is called **continental drift**.

This map shows the Earth's moving plates. It also shows active volcanoes. Many of these form mountains where the plates meet. You can see how volcanoes form on pages 10–11.

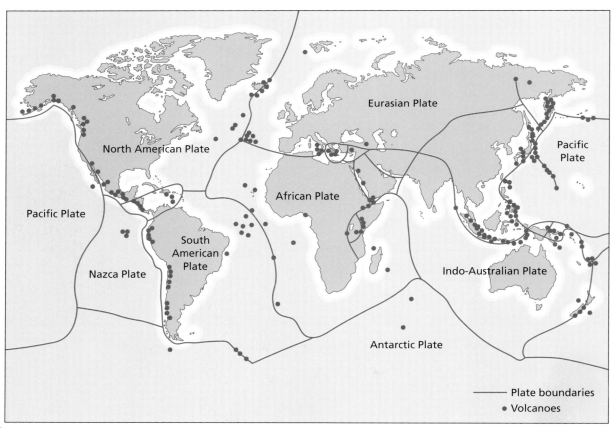

Eurasian Plate

North American Plate

Pacific Plate

Pacific Plate

African Plate

South American Plate

Nazca Plate

Indo-Australian Plate

Antarctic Plate

—— Plate boundaries
• Volcanoes

Fold mountains

Long ago, as the plates jostled together, they pushed the Earth's crust upwards. This crumpled the edges of continents. These became huge mountain **ranges** like the Himalayas and the Rockies.

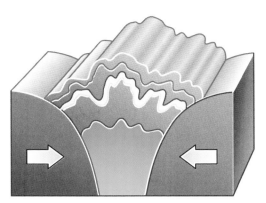

Fold Mountains

Block mountains

Movement under the Earth's crust also makes cracks in the rock, called **faults**. Blocks of rock slip up and down the faults, making some blocks rise above the others. These are known as block mountains. The Sierra Nevada range in the USA is caused by faulting.

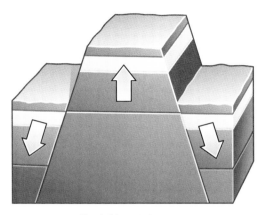

Block Mountains

Dome mountains

Dome-shaped mountains were formed when the Earth's movements pushed up hot, runny rock, called **magma,** from under the ground. The rock on the Earth's surface was too tough to crack open, leaving a dome shape. The Black Hills of South Dakota, USA, are dome mountains.

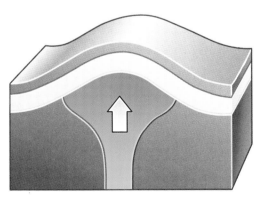

Dome Mountains

Worn mountains

Some mountains were made when soft rock got worn away by wind, rain, rivers and **glaciers** leaving areas of harder rock, high above the softer rock of the **valleys** and **plateaux**. The Ozark Mountains in the southern USA were formed like this.

Exploding mountains

Liquid mountains

Volcanic mountains occur where the Earth's crust is thin and weak. There are often earthquakes in these areas too, as you can see from the map on page 8. Volcanoes often begin with hot gases, ash and rocks exploding through cracks, called vents, in the Earth's surface. Hot **magma** rises from great chambers under the Earth's crust and then oozes out through the vent as well. When the magma reaches the air it cools and becomes **lava**, which is less runny than magma. The lava heaps up and cools further into a cone-shaped volcano with a huge hole at the top called a **crater**. Sometimes, lava is a bit thinner and runnier. It spreads out over a wider area, making a shield-shaped volcano with gently sloping sides.

Volcanoes can occur on land or under the ocean, where they often rise above the water as islands. The biggest volcano is the shield volcano called Mauna Loa. It lies on the main island of Hawaii in the Pacific Ocean. The tallest mountain in the world is a shield volcano.

Some volcanoes grow into mountains very quickly. This is Mount Paricutin in Mexico. It rises where there was once just a cornfield near a village. One day in 1943, smoke, ash and volcanic rocks suddenly spurted out of a crack in the ground. Then, burning orange lava gushed out. In just one week it built up into a hill 150 m high. Nine years later it reached a height of 410 m!

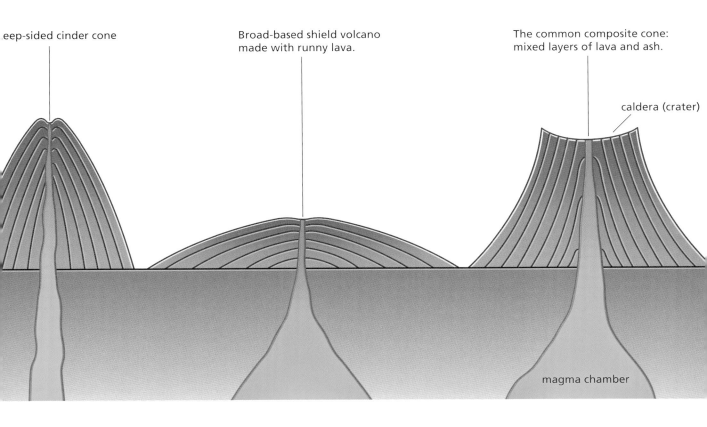

eep-sided cinder cone

Broad-based shield volcano made with runny lava.

The common composite cone: mixed layers of lava and ash.

caldera (crater)

magma chamber

It is Mauna Kea, which lies on the same island, although only 4205 metres of this mountain are above sea level.

Sleeping volcanoes

When a volcano has not erupted for millions of years it is called extinct, or dead. But a volcano that has not erupted for thousands of years is still thought to be alive. It is called dormant, which means that it is sleeping. Dormant volcanoes are very dangerous. Most have a **plug** of old, solid lava which fills the crater. When the volcano finally explodes again, enormous pressure builds up against the plug. This leads to a huge eruption. Mount St Helens in the USA lay dormant for 123 years. But, in 1980, magma pushed up against the solid rock and the pressure blew out a whole side of the mountain.

Volcanoes get worn down, just like any other mountain. When the soft layers of rock have been **eroded**, they leave a plug of hard, solid lava. Solid lava is often rich in **minerals**. Volcanic soils are very rich too. This is why farmers are attracted to the slopes of volcanoes. Volcanic craters often fill with water and become lakes.

11

What do mountains look like?

Mountains can have jagged **peaks** or flat tops. They can be a single colour, or bands of different coloured rock. It all depends on the age of the mountain, the kind of rock it is made from and how it has been **eroded**. Young mountain **ranges** have tall peaks and deep **valleys**, like the Alps in Europe. This is because there has not been enough time for **erosion** to flatten them. Older mountains have rounder peaks and shallower valleys. The Appalachians in North America are like this.

Sun, rain, frost and snow all wear down rocks. This is known as **weathering**. Rivers and **glaciers** carry away the pieces of broken rock. These bump against the mountain,

Erosion can reveal patterned layers of different types of rock, as you can see here in the Grand Canyon in the USA. But whole mountains can be made of just one type too. Some rocks have large crystals. Many of these are **igneous**, which means they are made of hardened **magma**. Others are smooth, such as marble. These are rocks that have been heated and pressed. They are called **metamorphic**. Softer rocks can be made of fine clays and gritty sand that were once covered in water. They are known as **sedimentary** rocks.

wearing it away even more. This kind of erosion is known as **corrasion**. The most powerful erosive force is a river. It can cut deep **gorges** between the mountains. Frost shatters rocks into lots of jagged pieces called **scree**. These are just pulled down the mountain by **gravity**.

But mountains are not just bare rock. Streams, waterfalls and small rivers run down them. Glaciers slip slowly towards the bottom. Small lakes fill dips in the rock, **scoured** out by the glaciers. Mountain peaks are often covered in snow, and snow-sheets cover flat slopes. Lower down, plant life colours the mountain green, except where the **climate** is very dry. Then, bare rock reaches right down to the valley floor.

This is called the 'Enchanted City'. It is in fact a type of rock called limestone that has been eroded into fantastic shapes. The 'city' lies in the Sierra de Valdecabras in Spain.

Weather on the mountains

You can often see clouds, rain and snow on mountains. Warm clouds are blown against the mountain and they rise up it. As the clouds rise, they cool in the chilly mountain air. This makes the **water vapour** in them turn into water droplets, which fall as rain high up on the mountain. The cold air also makes some of the rain fall as snow. On the other side of the mountain, the cold air sinks quickly. This can cause very strong air **currents**. These and other unusual weather features affect mountain life.

A great mountain range – the Rockies

The Rocky Mountains, or Rockies, are a long chain of mountain **ranges** stretching down the western side of North America. They were first folded upwards over 190 million years ago. They are still forming and rising. The chain has many different landscapes, from the **peaks** of Wyoming to the flat-topped rocks of the Grand Canyon. Most of the **erosion** has been caused by moving ice and water. There are wide **valleys scoured** out by **glaciers** and deep **gorges** carved by rivers. There are long ribbon-shaped lakes and hot volcanic springs. The

You can see from the map how the Rockies make a watershed between different river systems. For example, the great Colorado River flows westward from the Rockies into the Pacific Ocean. The waters of the mighty Missouri run eastward to the Mississippi River and eventually flow into the Gulf of Mexico, which opens out into the Atlantic Ocean.

Great Salt Lake sits in the middle of the Rockies' widest point. Its salty waters are due to **minerals** soaked from the rocks around it.

The chain passes through many different **climates** – from the frozen lands of Alaska in the north to hot, sunny Mexico in the south. The Rockies also affect the climate to the west. They stop rain from reaching it, making it into a dry rain-shadow area. But many rivers begin high up in the Rockies, which form a division, or **watershed**, between different river systems.

Life in the Rockies

Very small plants grow on most of the Rockies' peaks. Further down there are grasses and small shrubs. Below this lie huge forests, mainly of **conifer** trees, with grassland sloping away from them. The **vegetation** makes a good **habitat** for many different **species** of plant and animal.

There are about five million people living in the Rockies. Many live in mining towns and cities. The mountains are rich in minerals, such as gold, silver, copper, coal and iron ore. There is also natural gas and petroleum oil. Some people work in the forests, especially in the northern and Canadian Rockies. In the Colorado, Montana and Wyoming Rockies, farmers raise large herds of cattle and sheep. Many people are employed in tourism.

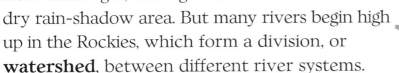

The Rocky Mountain National Park of the USA was created in 1915. It covers many peaks, 60 of which are over 3500 m high. Tourists can cross the park from east to west along Trail Ridge Road, which takes them over the Continental Divide. Deer, black bear, the Rocky Mountain Bighorn sheep, American elk and coyote roam the park. Golden eagles circle overhead. There are 700 species of plant, with carpets of wild flowers.

Mountain plants

Growing problems

The diagram below shows that there are different kinds of plant life in different mountain **climates**. But in all mountains, plants face the same problems. As the slope rises, the temperature cools. For every 150 metres of **altitude**, the temperature drops by about 1° Celsius. Plants also have to cope with big, quick temperature changes – from very cold at night to quite hot during the day. Mountain soils are thin and poor, and heavy rain high up makes any soil very wet. The soil often freezes too. Strong winds blow around and down the mountainside. Plants need sunlight to make their food and give them energy. But mountains are often shrouded in cloud.

Mountains in the far north or south are only able to support vegetation on their lower slopes.

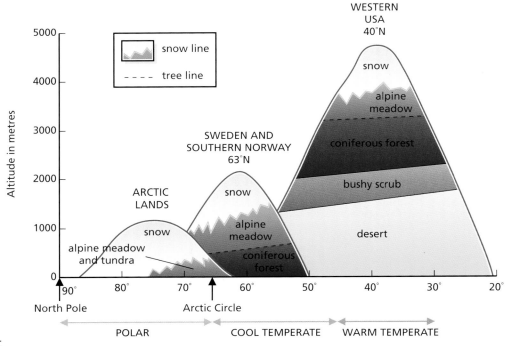

Tough plants

Plants have had to adapt to these harsh conditions. High up, tiny **lichens** cling to the bare rocks. Lichens are not true plants. They are a mixture of **fungi** and **algae**. But they are very tough and leathery and they do not need soil. Mosses are true plants but they are also very tiny. They, too, can cling fast and grow well in very damp conditions.

Lower down, larger plants often grow in sheltered cracks between the rocks, where there is often a little soil. They flower and produce seed in a very short time to avoid the long, harsh winters. Most mountain plants have very strong, clinging roots and short stems, which cannot break in the wind. Their leaves are small, flat and covered in hairs, spikes or spines. These let in warmth and light but stop the wind and ice from harming the leaf. The flowers are surrounded by leaves for protection. Grasses have a tough, waxy coating and are often bunched together like a bush. They sway in a rotating motion so they do not snap when the wind blows.

Mountains often have an area of **conifer** trees. Most conifer trees are evergreen, which means that they do not lose their leaves during the winter. This enables them to use even winter's weak rays of sun to make food. The leaves are thin and often spiky, with a waxy coating. This stops them from drying out when the trees' roots are unable to suck up moisture from frozen earth.

The silver fir grows in mountain forests in Europe – from the Pyrenees, through the Alps and eastward to the Balkan Mountains. Its wood is used for making boxes and for carving. It is also made into paper. Turpentine oil is extracted from the bark and mixed into paints. Turpentine from the leaves and wood is used in medicine for both humans and animals.

17

Mountain creatures

Mountain creatures have to survive in very harsh conditions, just like plants. There is less oxygen for animals to breathe high up in the mountains. This is because oxygen is a heavy gas which sinks. But many mountain **mammals** have developed large lungs and hearts to make the most of the small amount of oxygen available.

Many mammals live above the **tree line**. But in the bitter winters, some move from the **peaks** down to the **foothills**. Small mammals such as alpine marmots eat as much as they can during the summer. They store fat in their bodies and then **hibernate** in winter. The marmot hibernates in deep burrows which it fills with hay.

Mountain birds are usually large and strong, like this golden eagle, which is found in parts of Europe and North America. It has to fly in very fierce winds. The female golden eagle is larger than the male, and is about 1 m long from its beak to its tail. Its wings are 2 m wide when they are spread out. The eagle has very sharp eyes which help it to spot its prey from very high up. Strong talons grip small mammals and carry them away. The eagle eats meat, ranging from mice to young deer. Its nest is made from sticks and twigs, and is set high up on rocky mountain ledges.

But many mammals are adapted to the cold temperatures. Large mammals, such as the yak, llama and vicuna, often have thick, long fur. These shaggy coats trap air next to the animals' bodies, which heats the air and keeps them warm. The thick fur also protects them from the chill of the wind.

Mammals are often darkly coloured so they absorb the sun's weak rays. Pale colours would reflect more of the sun's heat and make the animal colder. But the Arctic hare and Arctic fox usually turn white in winter. This gives them **camouflage** against the snow. It protects the hare from being caught by **predators**. It stops the Arctic fox from being seen by its prey.

Mountain sheep, goats and small mammals feed mostly on tough grasses and small shrubs. But they can also eat **lichens** and mosses that cling to the rocks. The sheep and goats are able to climb on high, narrow ledges to find their food. The Rocky-Mountain goat has soft hoof pads with hard, sharp edges. These allow it to run on hard rock or ice, as well as soft snow.

The European brown bear lives in the mountains. They often make their homes in caves. Their long, shaggy coats protect them from the cold. But in the coldest part of winter the bear hibernates. Its temperature cools and its heartbeat slows down. This stops the bear from using up energy stored in its body fat.

Peoples of the mountains

Why do people live on cold, windy mountains? Thousands of years ago mountain caves made natural homes. They were easy to defend against enemies and wild animals. Some people still make their homes from caves. But today, cave dwellings have many modern facilities. The mountains provide wood and rock to build houses too.

Many mountain homes have small windows to keep out the cold. The roofs slope down over the sides of the house. This catches the snow and stops it from piling up against the walls.

Transport and communications are very difficult in the mountains. Road and railway tunnels and bridges have been made through the mountains to avoid the slopes. Cable cars carry people to higher parts of the mountain.

Food on the mountains

Many animals can be found above the **tree line**.
Sheep and goats provide mountain peoples with
meat, milk, wool and leather. Further down,
farmers raise larger herds of sheep and cattle
on the sloping grasslands. Crops of hay are also
grown there to feed the animals in the winter.

It is difficult to grow food crops on mountain
slopes. Soil is often poor and gets washed away
by the rain or blown away by the wind. Sometimes,
it is just pulled slowly down the slope by **gravity**.
This is known as soil creep. So farmers build flat
steps, called terraces, with long walls to keep in
the soil and water. Terraces are made in mountain
communities all over the world, from Peru to
China. Many kinds of crop can be grown on
terraces, from rice to grapes. Farmers grow an
even greater variety of crops on the rich soils
covering the slopes of volcanoes.

New Zealand sheep graze
high up in the mountains
during the summer. In the
autumn they are rounded up
and taken down to the
foothills. Some are sold
but the rest have to be
kept in the lowlands during
the winter. This movement
of animals is called
transhumance. It occurs in
the Himalayan **range**
and northern European
countries too.

A way of life – Tibet

Tibet is a land in central Asia hidden by mountains on three sides. These include the Himalayas and the world's highest mountain, Everest. Most Tibetans live on a very high **plateau** between the Karakoram Mountains in the west and the Kunlun range in the north. The average height of the land is about 4875 m above sea level. The region is known as the 'Roof of the World'.

The Tibetan people have adapted to the cold temperatures and thin air. They do not suffer from **altitude** sickness, which is caused by a lack of oxygen in the blood. More than this, Tibetans have used their natural **environment** to make a living and build their homes.

Many of Asia's most important rivers begin in the Tibetan mountains. The rivers include the Ganges, Indus, Brahmaputra, Mekong, Yangtze, Sutlej and Hwang-Ho.

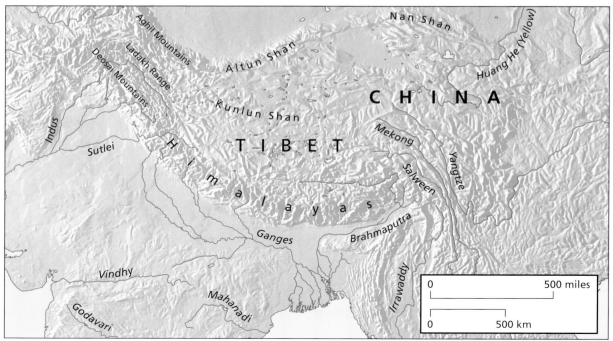

Making a living – building a home

Tibetan homes are made from mountain rock. They have thick walls and small windows to keep out the cold. But some Tibetans are nomads or partly nomads. This means that they travel with their herds of yaks, sheep and goats to find the best pastures. Cattle, horses and shaggy-coated Bactrian camels are also kept.

Tibetans grow barley, wheat, rye, fruit, vegetables and root crops such as potatoes on their farms. Cooking is often done outside on a stove made of stone, with a wood fire underneath. Tsampa is a favourite dish made of roasted barley seeds. Wheat flour is made into dumplings, which are stuffed with meat. Flour is also made into noodles.

Some Tibetans make a living as mountain guides to foreign tourists and climbers. They also carry the climbers' equipment for them. The mountains are full of **minerals** and gemstones, which Tibetans often use in jewellery. But mining has not yet become a big industry.

The yak is a very important animal for Tibetans. Yak meat is roasted, or dried to preserve it. The rich milk is made into butter, yoghurt, cheese and yak-butter tea, which can be drunk on its own or mixed with barley tsampa. Yaks can be many colours. This is because they are often mixed, or cross-bred, with cattle.

23

Our changing mountains

Natural changes

Mountains are changing naturally all the time. The Earth's **plates** are always moving apart or pushing together, making the mountains rise. Mountain blocks push up or slip down along the **faults** that lie in the Earth's crust. Hot **magma** continues to force its way to the surface, adding to existing volcanoes or making new ones.

Mountains are always being **eroded** too. This makes them continually change shape. The eroded material, such as fine soil and stones, gets swept down to the **valley** floor. This **sediment** then gets carried away by rivers to the sea. When it is in the water, the sediment builds up into layers of sandstone and clay rocks. These might one day be pushed or folded upwards into new mountains. And so the process begins again.

Bangladesh is a low-lying country in Asia. The great Rivers Brahmaputra and Ganges flow slowly through Bangladesh and into the sea. Once a year, very heavy rain falls down the mountains far away where the great rivers begin their course. This makes the rivers flood. The waters are usually welcomed, because farmers can plant rice and other crops in the flooded fields. But in recent years the waters have risen too high. This has been partly caused by cutting down too many trees in the mountains. The people of Bangladesh can do nothing about this problem, as the mountains lie in other countries.

Human changes?

The mountain **environment** has changed a lot, especially in recent times. Mining has cut great holes in the mountains. Many trees have been cut down from the forests too. This has left many mountainsides bare. It has destroyed the **habitat** of birds and **mammals**. The soil is no longer held together by the trees' roots, so it slips and washes down the slope. Rain cannot sink into the soil. It streams down the mountain and into the valley instead. This has led to more flooding in valleys.

There are also many more **avalanches**. Trees help to stop the snow from slipping, so cutting them down has partly caused the problem. So has **acid rain**, which has killed trees in many mountain forests. But some people think that avalanches are due to global warming. This is a change in **climate** that is slowly warming the Earth and melting the snow. Other people think that avalanches are caused by too many winter tourists skiing down the slopes.

You can see a lot of eroded material on this mountain. The stones and soil are called **scree**. This has happened naturally. It has altered the shape of the slope.

Looking to the future

The process of mountains being uplifted and **eroded** will never end. The forces that make and shape mountains are largely beyond our control. But we can help to look after the environment in the mountains and **valleys**. This will make them safe, healthy homes for plants, animals and humans alike.

A question of gas

We have seen on page 25 what effects global warming might be having in the mountains. But what are the causes of global warming and how can we stop it? Some scientists think that flares darting from the Sun are making the Earth hotter – we can do nothing about that. Others blame factories and car users

What is the future for people living in the Alps at Chamonix, in France? Chamonix is a very popular skiing resort. Buildings have been planned with safety in mind. There are concrete avalanche barriers 6 m high. But in February 1999 there were very heavy snowfalls – 2 m of snow fell in just a few days. This led to devastating avalanches. The worst avalanche hit buildings in what was thought to be a 'safe' area. At first, some people blamed tourists for skiing on dangerous slopes. But it seems that no one had been skiing there.

for burning too many **fossil fuels**, releasing harmful gases into the air. They also believe that CFC gases from refrigerators and aerosol cans have destroyed the protective **ozone layer** around the Earth. Fewer harmful gases will protect the Earth's ozone layer and help to solve the problem of **acid rain**, which is destroying many mountain forests.

Wearing away the mountains

Another problem is tree-felling, which has led to landslides, flooded valleys

and **avalanches** too. One of the solutions is to fell only older, mature trees and to replant with new trees straight away. This is now happening in many parts of the world.

Tourists are another big problem for mountain **environments**. Hikers and climbers are wearing away plants and soil on the mountain slopes. In parts of the USA, raised wooden walkways are used to protect the soil. More roads are also being built in the mountains to reach new tourist resorts. This is leading to soil erosion and landslides. Perhaps we could admire the mountains from a bit lower down!

◇ Empty oxygen bottles and plastic packaging litter climbers' base camps on Mt Everest. This kind of rubbish cannot dissolve and wash away. The problem of waste is growing on popular climbing peaks throughout the world.

Mountain facts

On top of the world

The Himalayas in central Asia has the 20 highest **peaks** in the world. The next highest mountains are found in the **belts** stretching through North and South America. The list below shows the highest peaks on different **continents**.

Continent	Mountain (Range)	Height above sea level
Asia	Everest (Himalayas)	8848 m
South America	Aconcagua (Andes)	6960 m
North America	McKinley (Rockies)	6194 m
Africa	Kilimanjaro (Northern Highlands, Tanzania)	5895 m
Oceania	Puncak Jaya (Pegunungan Maoke, New Guinea)	5029 m
Antarctica	Vinson Massif (Ellsworth)	4897 m
Europe	Mont Blanc (Alps)	4807 m

Did you know that satellite pictures are now used to measure the peaks of our tallest mountains? This makes the measurement more accurate. There have been many arguments about the height of Mt Everest!

Beneath the waves

The longest mountain range under the oceans is the India and East Pacific Oceans **Cordillera**. It is 19,000 km (12,000 mi) long.

This single peak is Mauna Kea, a volcanic mountain which lies mostly in the Pacific Ocean. It rises only 4205 m above the water. The other 5998 m are under the sea. Mauna Kea is the tallest peak in the world.

Not so steep

The smallest hill in the world is marked on official maps of Brunei, in Asia. It is only 4.5 m high and is part of a golf course!

Glossary

acid rain rain that has been polluted by gases rising from factories and motor vehicles

algae simple form of plant life, ranging from a single cell to a huge seaweed

altitude height of land above sea level

avalanche mass of snow that slips and hurtles down a mountainside

belt large group of mountain ranges (also called a cordillera)

camouflage colour or pattern that makes an object blend in with its surroundings

climate rainfall, temperature and wind that normally affect a large area

conifer tree that has cones to protect its seeds and normally keeps its spiny leaves throughout the year

continent the world's largest land masses. Continents are usually divided into many countries.

continental drift movement together or apart of the Earth's tectonic plates

cordillera large group of mountain ranges (also called a belt)

corrasion when stones get carried along by flowing water and bump against the river's bed and sides, eroding them away

crater hole or hollow in the top of a volcano

current strong surge of water that flows constantly in one direction in an ocean

environment natural and manmade things that make up our surroundings

erosion wearing away of rocks and soil by wind, water, ice or acid

fault crack deep in the Earth's crust

foothill any of the low hills around a mountain or mountain range

fossil fuels substances, including oil and gas, formed from the remains of animals that lived millions of years ago. They can be used as fuel.

fungus simple plant, such as a mould, mushroom or toadstool

glacier thick mass of ice formed from compressed snow. Glaciers flow downhill.

gorge narrow river valley with very steep sides

gravity force that causes objects to fall towards the Earth. We are all attracted to the Earth by gravity.

habitat place where a plant or animal usually grows or lives

hibernate when an animal hides away and sleeps during the winter. Its heart rate slows right down so its body uses less energy.

igneous crystal rocks made of hardened magma

lava less-runny magma that has reached the air above ground and has cooled

lichen not a true plant – a mixture of a fungus and algae

magma layer of hot melted rock beneath the hard crust of the Earth

mammal animal that feeds its young with its own milk

mantle layer of hot, molten rock on which the Earth's crust sits

metamorphic rocks that have been heated and compressed inside the Earth's crust

mineral substance that is formed naturally in rocks and earth, such as coal, tin or salt

ozone layer layer of gases, high up in the Earth's atmosphere, that protects us from the sun's harmful rays

peak highest point of a mountain

plate area of the Earth's crust separated from other plates by deep cracks. Earthquakes, volcanic activity and the forming of mountains take place at the junctions between these plates.

plateau area of high, flat ground, often lying between mountains

plug solid, tube-shaped piece of volcanic rock that fills a volcano when it dies or is dormant

predator animal that lives by feeding on other animals

range group of mountains formed at the same time and in a similar way

ridge long, narrow peak, range or watershed

scour rub hard against something, wearing it away

scree small, loose stones covering a mountain slope

sediment fine soil and gravel that is carried in water

sedimentary rocks made of layers of compressed clays and gritty sand that were once covered in water

species one of the groups used for classifying animals. The members of each species are very similar.

tree line highest part of a mountain on which trees can grow

valley scooped-out, low-lying area of land between mountains

vegetation the plants that grow in a certain area

watershed area of high ground surrounding a river's drainage basin

water vapour water that has been heated so much that it forms a gas which is held in the air – drops of water form again when the vapour is cooled. There is always water vapour present in the air.

weathering action of weather on rock or other materials

Index